Water in the Wilderness

T.D. Jakes

PNEUMA LIFE

PUBLISHING

Water in the Wilderness

T.D. Jakes

All Scripture quotation, unless noted otherwise, are from the holy Bible, King James Version.
Scripture quotations in this publication, unless otherwise noted, are taken from the Holy Bible: King James Version.

Printed in the United States of America
ISBN 1-56229-432-6

Pneuma Life Publishing
P.O. Box 10612
Bakersfield, CA 93389-0612
(805) 837-2113

Contents

About the Author
Dedication
Foreword
Introduction

Chapter   Page

Water in the Wilderness

Chapter One

Wilderness Before Inheritance

Jehoram the son of Ahab began to reign over Israel in Samaria the eighteenth year of Jehoshaphat king of Judah, and reigned twelve years. And he wrought evil in the sight of the LORD; but not like his father, and like his mother: for he put away the image of Baal that his father had made. Nevertheless he cleaved unto the sins of Jeroboam the son of Nebat, which made Israel to sin; he departed not therefrom.

And Mesha king of Moab was a sheepmaster, and rendered unto the king of Israel an hundred thousand lambs, and an hundred thousand rams, with the wool. But it came to pass, when Ahab was dead, that the king of Moab rebelled against the king of Israel. And king Jehoram went out of Samaria the same time, and numbered all Israel. And he went and sent to Jehoshaphat the king of Judah, saying, The king of Moab hath rebelled against me: wilt thou go with me against Moab to battle? And he said, I will go up: I am as thou art, my people as thy people, and my horses as thy horses. And he said, Which way shall we go up? And he answered, The way through the wilderness of Edom.

2 Kings 3:1-8

When you speak of the wilderness, your mind immediately imagines a dry place where nothing green grows. Everything in the wilderness is brown and unappealing to the eye. The environment of the wilderness is not brightened with any color. Everything in the wilderness has adapted itself to live in this type of climate. Rarely does it rain in the wilderness and when it does, plants store the moisture they need because there is no guarantee when it will rain again. When we are going through our wilderness experience, we must be like the trees and the other animals of the wilderness. We must learn to adapt our faith to the challenges a wilderness might bring.

The animals in the wilderness have learned to travel and hunt at night because it is cooler at night. Spiritually, we too must learn to find a place where the Lord can minister to us in our wilderness. It is a place where He can give us instruction about what to do next. Like the trees which store up water, uncertain of when it will rain again, we must store up His Word in our hearts. Many of us are living in the wilderness for various reasons.

The wilderness is a place of dying, where all the things that cause you to stumble in your walk with God are killed. If you have ever watched a movie where people dared to enter the wilderness, with little or no understanding of life in the wilderness, they often do not survive there. Since they had no one to help or advise them, they tried to fight the elements in their own strength.

Likewise, many of us have been in the wilderness and we have tried unsuccessfully to fight the battle in our own strength. You see, the wilderness is a place where God says, "I finally have you in a place where I can speak to you." As Jehoram was unprepared for life in the wilderness he needed someone who knew something about the wilderness. Hence, he asked for Jehoshaphat's help.

Do not be fooled into thinking that you can ever be fully prepared for life in the wilderness. Sometimes, God leads us abruptly into the wilderness. He might have been trying to get you to come to Him or to get you to take your spiritual life more seriously. Perhaps He has been trying to catch your attention to the call He has placed in your life.

It is indeed a gamble that the Lord takes on us for He knows that He cannot and will not override our will. But He also knows that it is truly our desire to do His will. Even the worst sinner is inwardly drawn to God even if he does not serve Him.

God loves you so much that He is willing to take just that type of risk on you. He knows that you may either serve Him or reject Him. You may say, "Lord, wherever you lead, I will follow, even through the wilderness." Or you may decide to say, "I can't deal with this. I thought life would be better than this, I quit."

But God knows that we must be tried in the fire so that we can become as pure as gold. God brings us into the wilderness to perfect our faith. You cannot have all pleasure without pain, neither can you enjoy only good times without adversity. Your faith is perfected in the furnace of affliction and adversity. There is something about going through dilemmas and crises that bring us to the place where we discover things about God which we would not have known under other circumstances.

The sins in Jehoram's life prevented him from walking with God like he should. His relationship with God was superficial. However, when he got in trouble he needed God as a fire escape. He called on God only when things were going bad. In essence, he wanted to use God as his servant, rather than serve God. He was interested in God only if God served his own selfish purpose.

Many of us have tried to use God for personal gain. We view God as a spiritual Santa Claus who is there at our every whim, one who will bring us gifts and presents that are beyond our reach. The only time we talk with Him is when we need something from Him.

If a loved one becomes terminally ill, we immediately call on Him. We are ready to beat down the pastor's door so that he can pray for us, or we call on the saints and implore their spiritual prayer and support. But, for some, as soon as the problem is over, what happens? We slum right back into the backslidden state we were in before the problem jolted us to pray. That is why many of us are constantly in problems.

God is fully aware of the sad fact that should we have all our needs met, we will never seek Him with all our hearts. Like the children of Israel, we tend to become arrogant, prideful, and forget the fact that we must fully acknowledge God in times of prosperity and adversity.

Jehoram was pretty smart, and he knew something about God. Realizing that he did not have a sound relationship with the Lord, he courted the friendship of one who did. He asked Jehoshaphat, king of Judah, "I have got to go out to fight and I want you to fight with me."

Jehoshaphat replied, "If you are going to war I will go with you. Your people are my people and I'm going to assume the responsibility of getting you the victory and all my captains and all my warriors are at your disposal." The next question was how to go about it.

But first, they must seek the mind of God on the matter. One of the servants of the king of Israel told Jehoshaphat about Elisha who had the word of the Lord. Jehoshaphat, Jehoram, and the king of Edom therefore travelled to see Elisha, the prophet. When he saw the three kings, he said to Jehoram, "What have I to do with thee? Get thee to the prophets of thy father, and to the prophets of thy mother.... As the LORD of hosts liveth, before whom I stand, surely, were it not that I regard the presence of Jehoshaphat the king of Judah, I would not look toward thee, nor see thee. 2 Kings 3:13-14

There are times, we are so obsessed with our destination that we forget that we must go through various phases to get there. For example when a woman is pregnant, it is apparent to all that she is carrying a baby. After the baby is born, all we see is a beautiful baby. We forget that there is a process of bringing that baby into the world - a process which is painful for both the mother and the child.

For the mother, it is the process of pushing this new delicate life out of her body where it has lived snugly for nine long peaceful months. For the baby, it is the process of being pushed into a place that it perceives to be unfriendly and cold, very different from the home it had occupied for the last nine months.

Just like the baby in its mother's womb, we may have to let go of something that has become part of us. We are always confessing that we want the perfect will of God for our lives, but we must not forget the fact that we must conquer the obstacles that stand in the way of our future success, in which God's ultimate will is realized.

King Jehoshaphat asked the question, "How shall we go up against Moab to get victory?" The unexpected answer was,

"You have to go through the wilderness of Edom to get the victory."

My friend, if you want to get to victory, you must be willing to go through the wilderness. I want to reiterate the fact it is not always easy to get to the victory because it belongs to the other side of the wilderness. You must be willing to go though a little time of abasement, confusion, adversity and even opposition before you arrive at your destination.

Many may think that it is unfair to go through this phase. But you see, it is the wilderness that weeds out the saints from the "aints." It is the wilderness that weeds out people who really want to do something for God, from people who just have a momentary superficial mundane relationship with Him. It is the wilderness that makes a hypocrite back up and say, "I can't take it anymore." The wilderness, God's killing field, will weed out all the impostors, because they cannot survive the adversity of the wilderness.

I want to warn you that you will have to go through the wilderness to attain the will of God for your life. The wilderness teaches us to stand; it teaches us to cast our cares upon Him. It teaches us to rely and totally depend on Him for life support, because we know in due season we shall reap if we faint not.

Some of us cannot handle the least problems. We feel that the hardships placed on our path indicates that God has either forsaken us, or that He is punishing us for some sin we have committed. But that is a lie which the devil has successfully employed to deter us from seeking the heavenly Father. Do not for a moment think that you can do it on your own. You will fail woefully.

Remember Joshua and Caleb. Had they tried to enter the Promise Land on their own strength or cognizance, they would have perished in the wilderness. Even when life in the wilderness became dull and unappealing, they did not stop seeking God neither did they cease to rely on His guidance. Like Joshua and Caleb, we must be persistent in faith even in the wilderness where problems are at their peak.

The greatest battle that we face while we are in the wilderness is the one between the new and the old man. The old man that God is trying to kill in the wilderness refuses to die. It wants to resurrect old hurts and old problems. But, as new creatures in Christ Jesus, the old man must be put to death. You must constantly remind yourself that you are a new creature despite the situations you are facing, and that the **old man** is **DEAD!!**

Chapter Two

Who is Your God?

Jesus answered and said, "It is written you shall worship the Lord your God and him only shalt thou serve:" Luke 4:8b

My God is the Alpha and the Omega, the Beginning and the End. There is nothing too hard for Him. There is nothing He cannot handle. Because we know who we are in Christ Jesus and what we mean to our Heavenly Father, Satan tries to discourage us. He tries to use sickness, financial problems, family stress: and anything and everything you can think of to incapacitate us. The question you must ask yourself is, "Who is my God? Who do I serve?" Then answer the question, "My God is the way Maker." The Bible says that if God be for us, who can be against us. (Romans 8:3)

God is so real in my inward man. He has not only washed away all my sins, but He has filled my cup with His love, that my cup bubbles over. He is the Lover of my soul; He is the Answer to my every need; He is my burden Bearer. Maybe you are the kind that can handle everything that comes your way, but I can't. However, I know someone who is able to make it. His name is Jesus Christ.

The enemy fights those who know who they are and whose they are. The Bible affirms that God is faithful (1 Cor. 1:9) The Word of God states, "But to us there is but one God the Father, of whom are all things, and we in Him; and one Lord Jesus Christ, by whom are all things, and we by Him" (1 Cor. 8:6).

Are you aware that the more the enemy fights you, the greater the indication that blessings are on the way? You must be cognizant of this fact as a Christian. If you do not know that about life, you cannot make it. You have got to know that it is because you are on the verge of a miracle that the devil is fighting you. He is fighting you so hard because you are getting closer to your deliverance, and the greater you get the greater the struggle.

If you hold out a little while longer, God's going to give you the victory in every circumstance of your life. I am learning to be encouraged when I meet with obstacles because I see them as an indication of a fresh move of God in my life.

Therefore when people ask you who your God is, you can with confidence, shoulders high and a smile on your face say, "He is everything I will ever need. He is my Father, the Creator of heaven and earth, and the One who sustains the universe. He is Jehovah, the I am, that I am."

Water in the Wilderness

Chapter 3

God's Got A Plan

When you are in the wilderness you must find out what the plan of God is for you. You cannot rely on anyone else's plan. Only a plan from God will suffice in the wilderness.

God has not promised that you will not go through hardship, neither has He promised you that you will not experience adversity. But listen to what He says, "When you pass through the waters I will be with you, and when you go through the flood I'll be there and should you have to go through fire, I will be there. As I was with Shadrack, Meshack and Abednego, so will I be with you. I will be the fourth One in the furnace."

I am very grateful that the Lord's been walking with me all these years. I say this not because I have not been through anything, or that I have not faced various challenges and dark moments in life, but I do recognize that the Lord has been the fourth One in the fiery furnace. He has protected me from the scorching of the flames. When the pressure and the flame seem as if they would engulf me, His words of assurance would comfort me.

There are many who would have lost their mind had the Lord not been on their side. They would have gone crazy and lost control, but the Lord comforted them in their darkest hour. It is not that we did not go though the wilderness but when we went through it, God was with us. God will be with you when mama, daddy, sister and brother leave. When the folks you thought would be with you all the way, walk out of the door, God says, "Lo, I am with you always even unto the ends of the world."

You need not fear the wilderness if you take God with you everywhere you go. I must take Him with me everywhere I go, or else I would fall on my face. I truly need the Lord for I cannot function without Him. I need Him in the morning; I need Him in the noon day; I need Him when the sun is down. I need Him to run my business; I need Him to teach me how to be a good father; I need Him to be a good husband. Don't you try to be anything without God, because you will not succeed.

The enemy may come to discourage you. He may whisper to your mind that God will not help you or that you might have committed a horrible sin which has brought God's wrath on you. Satan thinks that he catches the Lord by surprise. But, oh, is he wrong! God is a God of plans. He is a God of order. As the God who knows all things, He is never surprised by the attack of the enemy. While the enemy is planning his strategies, God has already made a counter plan for him. He has already made a way of escape for you. Yes, you must trust Him.

Peter asked the Lord Jesus if he could join Him on the sea. After the Lord told him to come, Peter got out of the boat, and walked on the sea until he removed his eye off of Jesus.

Maybe you are in trouble right now. Maybe you are reading this book, trying to find answers to your situation. Maybe you have been trying to run your life without God or you have been trying to deal with your wilderness without God's help. You may be convinced you know what you are doing and that you are not obligated to listen to anyone. Be careful, for pride comes before a fall. My friend, you do need God. You need Him to help you to hold your mind together.

You need Him when you are at the breaking point and people have disappointed you. Nobody else but God will get up with you at 3:00 in the morning, and hold you in His arms. Nobody else but God can comfort you when you are depressed. Only God can supernaturally soothe your nerves and quell your worries. Only He can give you that peace that passes all understanding. When the Scripture talks about the peace that passes all understanding, it is referring to a peace that is anointed. When people look at your situation, and then look at you, they will be confused. They would say, "Why is he so peaceful? Doesn't he realize that he has nothing, and everything he had is gone? Why is he so peaceful? It is simply the God-given peace which he is enjoying. Try it, and believe me you will like it. God says "It's going to be alright. Just trust me, just lean on me, and look to me for total deliverance."

You might not be able to see how it will work out, but you've got to trust that before it is all over with, God's going to give you the victory. You see, God's got a plan!

Water in the Wilderness

Chapter 4

The Power of Praise

I will bless the Lord at all times: His praise shall continually be in my mouth. My soul shall make her boast in the LORD, the humble shall hear thereof, and be glad. O magnify the Lord with me, and be glad and let us exalt his name together. I sought the Lord, and he heard me, and delivered me from all my fears. They looked unto him, and were enlightened: and their faces were not ashamed.

Psalms 34:1-5

Praise is magnifying and exalting the Lord in our hearts. Praise is glorifying the Lord with the fruit of our lips. When we begin to praise God with all our heart, we lose sight of the magnitude of our problems as we gain a vision of the greatness of our Lord.

In order to truly praise God, we must learn to go beyond ourselves and our human limitations. Many times when the enemies of Israel would encamp around them, they would tell Joshua to send out the tribe of Judah first. Judah means praise. Judah would go out before the enemies of Israel, armed with nothing but instruments of PRAISE.

When the tribe of Judah would begin to praise God with their whole heart, God would set ambushment among the enemy, and confuse them. The same principle happens in the spirit realm. When we really begin to praise God, our praise literally confounds the enemy, and demonic forces begin to withdraw their power and influence.

For though we walk in the flesh we do not war after the flesh: For the weapons of our warfare are not car-

nal but mighty though God to the pulling down of strongholds; Casting down imaginations, and every high thing that exalteth itself against the knowledge of God, and bringing into captivity every thought to the obedience of Christ.
2 Cor. 10:3-4

Praise and worship is the most profound way of expressing our love to the Father. God loves to be praised and worshipped. However, in order to praise God, we must understand the power that praise and worship wield. Praise and worship can break demonic strongholds that have bound some of us.

Praise and the Word of God are able to pull down strongholds. There is power in praise and worship. Let us pause here to examine this spiritual concept of praise as a weapon against spiritual strongholds.

First, let us define strongholds. Strongholds are road blocks or stumbling blocks that prevent God's people from truly releasing themselves in praise and worship to God. There are several strongholds but we will only talk about one. The erection of strongholds take place in our thought-process.

For example, suppose you were visiting a new church where their method of praise and worship is somewhat different from yours. Immediately, your mind tells you that their way is wrong, or worse still, that they are not saved. This is a stronghold. Remember that a stronghold is a belief system that is contrary to what Gods' Word says. You see, in this case, your church has spoken against being too expressive in worship and praise. To them praise and worship does not have to be loud and noisy.

I have noticed that many people in the church do not know how to worship or praise the Father. We get nervous when someone during service gets too loud and starts to worship God differently from our normal style. We want to worship God in low voices and that's only on Sunday mornings in our lofted buildings. We must appear "respectable." But in the clubs at baseball or football games, the same people will yell and make as much noise as they can without getting the least nervous or losing their "respectability."

The Lord loves to hear us praise His holy name and doesn't get nervous when we either become too loud or too quiet. It is we who discriminate about how to praise God. We must be very cautious about this area of our lives. If we allow Satan to build up strongholds we create more road blocks in our minds that prevent us from praising God freely. Someone once said, "a free person is a dangerous person because they do not allow anyone to dictate what they say or do except the LORD!"

Once the believers understand how Satan uses strongholds to keep them from releasing themselves in praise and worship, they are better prepared to use their weapons of praise and worship. Someone once said, "We must understand that the area of thoughts is both the first and final battlefields. It begins with the mind before it goes to any other area." Hence, Satan fights us in our minds to such great extent.

What is Praise?

Praise is replacing your thoughts and the enemy's thoughts with the thoughts of God. The Word of God, the Name of Jesus, and the Blood of Jesus are weapons of God that transform and change our thoughts. Although many people may not realize this truth, a tremendous amount of power is released when praise is offered to God. This is a weapon that is often taken for granted. Imagine what David felt as he composed his Psalms. When you take God's thoughts and enter into praise, you become like a battering ram against the strongholds that Satan has erected in your mind.

Another stronghold that we must pull down is the idea that the believer should look sad and gloomy whenever he is going through a difficult time. We think that the devil is having his hey day with us, using us like a dust rag; This ought not to be. We must speak God's Word over the state of our emotions. It is indeed possible to change the state of your mind through the Word of God. Satan tries to destroy you through your mind. Allow the Lord to direct you.

Have you ever heard the voice of God through the thick of the night and thereby you get your victory? It wasn't because you were smart; it wasn't because you were taught; it wasn't because you were so good, but maybe just because you learned how to say, "Lord, I love you, I praise you, I'm in trouble, but I still love you." "I have trials, but I still love you." "I don't feel good this morning, but I still love you." "I have bills I can't pay, but I still love you." David said, "I will bless the Lord at all times."

Music and Praise

But now bring me a musician. And it happened when the musician played, that the hand of the Lord came upon him. 2 Kings 3:15

Elisha requested for a musician because he saw the need for music. We too need some music in the church. Music has the ability to change attitudes and emotions within us. It has the ability to mold and shape thoughts. We have an assortment of instruments - drums, tambourines, organs, and pianos. One king obtained the victory just because he had an orchestra with him. The musicians of the temple of the Lord played musical instruments until the enemy of Israel became confused and started killing one another.

God loves music. He said, "If you want me to move, play me some music. Get me somebody who has got an instrument." When Saul was possessed with demons, David would play on his harp until the demons leaped out of Saul. There is something about the anointed music of the Holy Spirit.

Anointed music will drive out demons, trouble and sickness. That is why you must be very careful about the type of music that you allow to enter your soul for it has a great effect on your inner man (spirit man). Get some anointed and powerful music. If you want your body to be healed, get some music that speaks healing into your body. Elisha said, "Get me somebody who will play me a song." The Bible says that when the minstrel began to play, the Word of the Lord began to flow out of Elisha's mouth.

Don't you allow anyone to take your song from your lips. You may lose friends, but don't lose your song. You might not sing well in the hearing of other people, but keep your song. You might croak like a frog, but keep your song. David said, "Make a joyful noise unto God, all ye lands" (Psalms 66:1). Paul demonstrated that if you have a song, you can sing your way out of the jail. If you have a song, you can encourage yourself. Even when there is nobody around to encourage you, and you feel all alone, if you have a song you can encourage yourself in the Lord.

God will move when you start praising Him. When you start to praise God,

He will come in the middle of your drought, in the middle of your wilderness and in the middle of your dry place, and say, "I've got a plan!"

Chapter 5

Intimacy in Worship

**Thou shalt worship the Lord thy
God, and Him shall thou serve.
Matthew 4:10**

Whatever we worship is what we ultimately will end up serving. Our nature demands that we worship something. What we worship is up to us.

**But the hour cometh, and now is,
when the true worshippers shall
worship the Father in spirit and in
truth: for the Father seeketh such
to worship Him. John 4:23**

To experience true worship you must first develop a relationship with the Father. All relationships are dependent upon good communication. For us as believers, prayers is the means of communicating with the Father. This relationship can be likened to that of a man and his wife. There is the sense of intimacy, closeness, and oneness. It is the closeness that you should never share with anyone else.

When a man and a woman first get married, their relationship is new and exists on that level of looking deeply into each other's eyes. This is the honey moon stage. At this stage, the couple worships the ground that the other walks on. Their focus is on each other. But, as time goes on, the honey dries a little and the moon begins to lose its lustre. The newness in their relationship begins to wear off, giving way to a different dimension in their relationship.

They begin to know each other on a more intimate relationship. They can feel each other's hurts and desires. They avoid what will hurt each other or that would jeopardize their closeness. They don't hide anything, rather, they express their feelings in confidence and trust. They trust each other with their weaknesses and short-comings, confident that they would not be used against them. This is the kind of desire that the Lord wants us to enjoy with Him, a close relationship that leads to intimate worship.

There are different kinds of gods we may find ourselves bowing to. Some of us worship our children. Some worship money. Some worship sin. Some worship themselves while others worship all types of things, ... paycheck, reputation etc.

Have you ever observed a Christian who recently got saved? He worships God with a deep gratitude for his salvation. The first stage in the romance of a man and woman is often referred to as infatuation. This is also typical of the first stage of our relationship with Christ. Dictionary describes infatuation as "to behave foolishly, to inspire with foolish and unreasoning love or attachment." However, as we mature in the Lord, this type of attraction takes on a new and higher dimension. Infatuation, like romance, operates more on feelings than reality, on the external than on the internal. It is more fleeting than stable, more inconsistent than constant. But the mature love is consistent because it is based on commitment. Commitment (covenant) is what sustains any lasting and stable relationship.

When a man first falls in love with a woman, it might have been her beauty and figure that attracted him. But after the marriage, and he wakes up in the morning to bad breath, hair rollers or even to the body that has birthed two or three children, infatuation finds its way out through the window. It is neither infatuation nor romance that keeps him coming home, but the commitment to the vow that he made at the altar that sustains the relationship.

The same commitment must define our relationship with the Lord. We must graduate from the point where we praise and worship God only for what He does for us, but we praise Him for who He is. Our worship must transcend a superficial expression that is dependent on our feelings alone. We must develop a relationship that is consistent even in the midst of trials. The trials should deepen our relationship with the Lord, not weaken it.

Wilderness experiences will mature our relationship with the Lord to the degree that our worship is expressed not only externally by the fruit of our lips in praise, but also our love for Him expressed through our continual obedience. It is the obedience that flows from the heart, freely without coercion.

Water in the Wilderness

Chapter 6

No Wind, No Rain, Just Water

For thus saith the Lord, Ye shall not see wind, neither shall ye see rain, yet that valley shall be filled with water, 2 Kings 3:17

Can you still believe this promise after all you have been through - with all your suffering, and deprivation of winds and rain? God said He is going to give you the water. Since the king of Moab did not see rain, he apparently did not expect to see water. And when he came upon the mountain top, and looked down in the valley, the ray of the sun on the water gave the appearance of blood. He thought it was the blood of his enemies.

He ran down there to kill them, but what he thought was blood was just water.

Some of you should have been dead and long gone, but God saw your blood and sent you the water. You could have died of spiritual dehydration, but He did not send wind or rain, just water. You could have given up, but you did not give up. I could have passed out, but I am not out. There is water in my family, water in my relationships, water in my church, water in my preaching, water in my business, water in my home, water in my career, water, water, water, water... water everywhere.

There are some people in the wilderness who don't have any water yet, and unless they have someone to minister to them as Elisha ministered to Jehoshaphat and Jehoram, they will die in the wilderness without water. Someone must preach the gospel until their dry areas are made wet. You don't have to give up, you don't have to give in, you don't have to quit. God said He will fill those dry areas of your life with water.

If you have been going though dry places and wilderness for a long time, God is saying, "Dig some ditches, because I'm getting ready to bless you and your latter day is going to be greater than your former day." God will fill the ditches in your homes and marriages with water. To the ditches of finances, God says "I will fill them with water." To the ditches of your emotions, He says, "Get your mind ready, get your attitude right, get your heart fixed, because when I open up the windows of heaven I am going to pour you out a blessing that you will not have room enough to receive."

It is a blessing that will be pressed down, shaken together, and running over. Are you ready for the blessing? Some people may be thinking of quitting, but don't quit. The moment that you are ready to throw in the towel, when you think you cannot take it any more, it is then that God will send you His blessing. Do not allow Satan to discourage you and thus deprive you of God's blessing. The devil is a liar and the father of lies.

God repeats,, "Dig ditches in your valley." Get ready! You have been suffering for a long time, but I am getting ready to bless you. I want you to dig ditches and get ready. As soon as you are ready, the answer will be there. When the answer comes, it is going to come in the spirit and not in the flesh. Once the ditches have been dug, there will be no warning or sign, no clouds, no winds, not even rain, just water.

In the natural when it is about to rain, one can tell by the wind and the cloud, but God is saying, "I'm going to send you a blessing that has no sign, and it will not have any warning. Everything may be stagnant, but I am going to move in the midst of your stagnation. Just because you do not see any wind does not mean that I am not getting ready to bless you. Get ready!!!

You might look up and not see any sign in the climate. Maybe, you do not see the clouds forming in the sky. I know you are use to lightening, but there might not be any. I know that you are use to thunder before the outpouring, but you may not hear the thunder. There might not be wind. It might not even rain, but just because there is no wind, nor rain, does not mean that there won't be water."

You must know that God is going to bless you. I can care less if the wind is not blowing or the thunder is not sounding, you must know the God cannot lie. If He has promised to bless you, then He will bless you. If He has promised to deliver you, then He will deliver you. If He has promised to bring you out, then He is able. The Lord is more than able. No wind, no rain, but there will still be blessing without warning. You must expect the blessing to come.

When God was ready to send the flood, He did not just send water down on Noah. The Bible says that He broke up the cisterns of the deep, and water started coming up out the of the ground. (Gen. 7:11) Yes, water started coming out of the dry places.

Do you have any dry places? God is saying that is where the water is going to come from. Have you had struggles in any areas of your life? God says that is where the water is going to come from. Do you have frustrations? God says He is going to send the water out of your pain and agony.

Maybe the water is trickling at first. Have you ever said, "I'm getting something, but that is not enough. I am better than what I used to be, but I still don't have that break-through. I am not saying that you are not blessing me Lord, but something is missing out of my blessings. I am getting a little moisture." But God is telling you now to wait on Him. You must learn how to wait. It is they that wait upon the Lord whose strength God will renew.

The Word of God says to wait. Wait even when it seems that nothing is happening. Wait while you are in the midst of the wilderness, when there is no sign of water. Wait on the perfect timing of

God. Remember that He has a plan. He has not forsaken you even though the devil might have given you the impression that He has. As you wait, the Lord says, "Mount up with wings like eagles, run and don't be weary, walk and don't faint because that little drip of water is turning into a trickle, and the trickle will turn to a stream, and the stream will turn to a creek, the creek is going to turn to a lake, and the lake is going to turn to a river.   And out of your belly, as the Word says, will flow rivers of living water."

God will send you some water that will come out of your wilderness, and when it comes, it will be more than enough. If you do not have wind, do not worry. If you do not see rain, do not be perturbed. God is still going to give you the water. If you want the outpouring of God's Spirit, wait for Him. God will send you water in your dry places. God will send the water right into your personal wilderness.

Water in the Wilderness

Chapter 7

Water in the Wilderness

And all the congregation of the children of Israel journeyed from the wilderness of Sin, after their journeys, according to the commandment of the LORD, and pitched in Rephidim: and there was no water for the people to drink. And the people thirsted for water; and the people murmured against Moses, and said, Wherefore is this that thou had brought us up out of Egypt, to kill us and our children and our cattle with thirst? And the LORD said unto Moses, Go on before the people, and take with thee of the elders of

Israel; and thy rod, wherewith thou smotest the river, take in thine hand and go. Behold I will stand before thee there upon the rock in Horeb; and thou shall smite the rock, and there shall come water out of it, that the people may drink. And Moses did so in the sight of the elders of Israel. Exodus 17: 1, 3, 5-6.

There is water in the wilderness. If you are going through the dry places, is it not wonderful to know that God is a cool drink while in a hot and thirsty land? When you run out of water, run out of friends, run out of ideals and run out of plans, God says, "You are going through a tough time, but do not worry; I have a plan."

God has a way of escape. I do not know what wilderness you are going through, but I do know this much about God: He will step over into the middle of the wilderness of your dilemma. He is not confined to the church building. He is also God in your wilderness.

He will come into your house. He will come on your job. He will take care of you. Have you ever found yourself praising God in the car, and the praise reaches a height where tears swell up your eyes, and you know you must stop the car for fear that you might hit someone? Have you been in a situation where you are worshipping God, and people around you thought that you were talking to yourself.

Has the Lord ever visited you in an awkward place? A place such as the bus stop, or a subway where you really do not have the freedom to praise God. However, the praise got so high within you that it took every muscle of your will power to keep quiet.?

I enjoy being by myself with God. If I shout too loud in the public, and the people get nervous, I cannot be very free. But when I am alone, I can call on God as loud as I want, and I can cry as long and as loud as I want to cry. If I want to pat my foot, I can pat my foot. If I feel like moaning, I can lay out and moan without the fear that someone is commenting about it. When I wave my hands, He understands.

You may be in a dry place where there is no water. Or you may be in the wilderness or in a deep valley, but remember, God provides water in the dry places.

When I was in Arizona last year on a preaching tour, I had a chance to see a dry bed river. As I walked down into the dry river bed I sensed in my spirit that the Lord was ministering to me about this dry river bed. Once there was water in the river bed, but now it had gone dry. Yet, you could still tell that there used to be water there, but due to the dryness in the atmosphere, it had dried up. It is amazing that the sun was able to absorb that much water. The rocks could still be seen at the bottom of the river bed. Yet there was no life there.

Unfortunately, this is the way some churches are today. There once was water in these churches. There used to be some glory in their midst. The church use to be spiritually alive, but now there is no sign of life.

A principle needs to be underscored here. If the river dried up over here, then you must go over there. If you are going through a dry time in your life, then you must find water. If you do not find some water, you will be like those animals that died without water.

I am conscious of the fact that I need some water every hour of the day. I am not in need of someone who would beat me over the head with the Word just to make me feel bad, but I do need someone who can tell me that I can make it. I need someone to tell me that God is my deliverer, that He is my Joy in the midst of sorrow, that the He is my Healer, the One who makes a way where there seems to be none.

I need someone to tell me He is a strong Tower, that He is the Doctor in the sick room, the lawyer in the courtroom and the Water in the wilderness. God says, "This is what I want you to do while you are still down in the dry river bed: dig ditches in your valley." Now it may seem to me that it would have been enough for God to fill your river bed, but God says He is going to bless you much more than the river bed can contain.

You had better begin to dig those ditches in the river bed, because what you need is not deep enough for my supply, and when I do bless you, my blessing is going to be so much greater than your present capacity to receive. So dig some ditches for the outpouring. Contrary to how bleak and distraught the situation may be or how devastating the trial or crisis, remember God has said, **"I will Provide Water in the Wilderness."**

Water in the Wilderness

Book

Water in the Wilderness

God's Provision For Your Every Need

by T.D. Jakes

Just before you apprehend your greatest conquest, expect the greatest struggle. Many are perplexed who encounter this season of adversity.

This book is designed as a map. (1) It will show you how to survive the worse of times with the greatest of ease; (2) It will cause fountains of living waters to break forth out of the parched, sun drenched areas in your life. This word is literally a stream in the desert. To the weary traveler I say; Come and drink!

$5.95

To order toll free call:
T.D. Jakes Ministries
1-800-BISHOP-2

Book

Why?
Because Your Are Anoited
by T.D. Jakes

Why is it that the righeous, who have committed their entire lives to obeying God seem to endure so much pain and experience such conflict? These are perplexing questions that plagued and bewildered Christians as well as unbelievers for ages. In this anointed and inspirational new book. "WHY," Bishop T.D. Jakes, the preacher with the velvet touch and explosive delivery, provoctvely and skillfully answers these questions and many more as well as answering the "WHY" of the Anointed.

$6.95

**Use order form to
order directly from:
T.D. Jakes Ministries**

Book

Woman , Thou Art Loosed
by T.D. Jakes

This book offers healing to hurting single mothers, insecure women, and battered wives,; and hope to abused girls and women in crises! Hurting women around the nation-and those who minister to them-and devouring the compassionate truths in Bishop T.D. Jakes' Woman, Thou Art Loosed.
Retail $8.95
Also available as a workbook
Retail $5.95

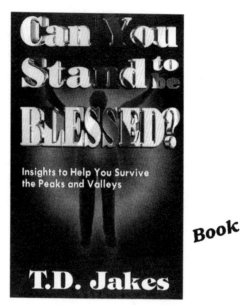

Book

Can You Stand to Be Blessed
by T.D. Jakes

Does any runner enter a race without training for it? Does a farmer expect a harvest without preparing a field? Do Christ6ians believe they can hit the mark without investing any effort?

In this book T.D. Jakes teaches you how to unlock the inner strength to go on in God. The requirements that he discusses prepare you for your intended purpose. The only question that remains is, *Can You Stand to Be Blessed*?

Retail $8.95

**Use order form to
order directly from:
T.D. Jakes Ministries**

Video

MANPOWER

Healing the Wounded Man Within

Wounded men will experience the transforming power of God's Word in Manpower. Satan has plotted to destroy the male, but God will raise up literally thousands of men through this life-changing, soul-cleansing, and mind-renewing word. This 4-part audio series is for every man who ever had an issue he could not discuss; for every man who needed to bare his heart and had no one to hear it.

To order toll free call:
T.D. Jakes Ministries
1-800-BISHOP-2

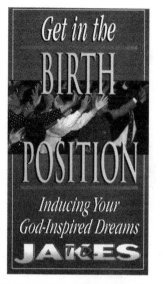

Video

GET IN THE BIRTH POSITION
Inducing Your God-Inspired Dreams

God's Word is steadfast. Nothing can stop what God has promised from coming to pass. However, you need to get ready. In this message T.D. Jakes shares the steps necessary to bring to birth the promises of God in your life.

**Use order form to
order directly from:
T.D. Jakes Ministries**

THE 25TH HOUR
When God Stops Time For You!

Have you ever thought, "Lord I need more time"? Joshua thought the same thing, and he called upon the sun and moon to stand still! This message from Joshua 10 testifies of the mightiness of our God, who can stop time and allow His children to accomplish His purposes and realize the victory!

To order toll free call:
T.D. Jakes Ministries
1-800-BISHOP-2

THE PUPPET MASTER

The vastness of God, His omnipotence and omnipresence, His working in the spirit world-these are concepts difficult to grasp. In this anointed message, T.D. Jakes declares God's ability to work for your deliverance, for He can go where you cannot go, do what you cannot do, and reach what you cannot reach!

Use order form to order directly from: T.D. Jakes Ministries

**TELL THE DEVIL
"I CHANGED MY MIND!"**

The scriptures declare that it is with the mind that we serve the Lord. If there was ever a battleground that Satan wants to seize and dominate in your life, it's right in the arsenals of your own mind. We must get the victory in our thought-life.

I believe that even now God is calling every prodigal son back home. Both the lost and the lukewarm are being covered and clothed with His righteousness and grace. I pray that this life-changing, soul-cleansing, mind-renewing message will help you find your way from the pen back to the palace.

**To order toll free call:
T.D. Jakes Ministries
1-800-BISHOP-2**

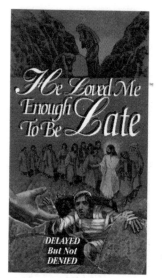

Video

HE LOVED ME ENOUGH
TO BE LATE
Delayed But Not Denied

Many of us have wondered, "God, what is taking
you so long?" Often God doesn't do what we
think He will, when we think He will, because He
loves us. His love is willing to be criticized to
accomplish its purpose. Jesus chose to wait until
Lazarus had been dead four days, and still raised
him up! This message will challenge you to roll
away your doubt and receive your miracle from
the tomb!

**Use order form to
order directly from:
T.D. Jakes Ministries**

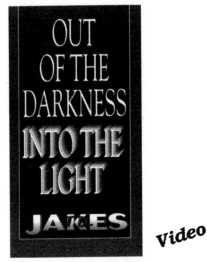

Video

OUT OF THE DARKNESS
INTO THE LIGHT

When Jesus healed a blind man on the sabbath by putting mud on his eyes and telling him to wash, He broke tradition in favor of deliverance. That is the example the Church must follow. Are we willing to move with God beyond some of the things we have come from? Can we look beyond our personal dark moments to God? The Light of the world is ready to burst into our lives!

**To order toll free call:
T.D. Jakes Ministries
1-800-BISHOP-2**

Video

THE KINGDOM IS GOING TO THE DOGS

Join Bishop Jakes as he delivers one of the most startling revelations of our time — that God is going to give the very best to the very least. The blessings of the Lord are going to come upon people that others thought would never be used. Those who have been through traumas and tragedies are now being groomed for greatness and authority.

Find out what you have to do to line up with what God has prepared for you. The blessing is not going to come to those who thought they deserved it; the Kingdom is going to those who have considered themselves unworthy. The Kingdom is going to the dogs.

Use order form to
order directly from:
T.D. Jakes Ministries

Cassettes, Books and Videos from
T.D. Jakes

Cassettes Series

The Gates of Hell	$20.00
Lord Save Our House	$20.00
When Helping You is Hurting Me	$20.00
Woman Thou Art Loosed (Part 1)	$20.00
Woman Thou Art Loosed (Part 2)	$20.00
Loose That Man & Let Him Go (Pt 1)	$20.00
Loose That Man & Let Him Go (Pt 2)	$20.00
MANPOWER:	$20.00

Healing The Wounded Man Within

Books

Why?	$6.95
Water in the Wilderness	$5.95
Woman Thou Art Loosed	$8.95
Can You Stand to Be Blessed	$8.95
First Lady	$20.00
Give The Man What He Wants	$20.00
The Spell Is Broken	$20.00
Turning Pressure into Power	$20.00

Audio	Video
Woman Thou Art Loosed (Azusa '93)	
$6.00	$20.00
Get in The Birth Position	
$6.00	$20.00

Audio	Video
The 25th Hour	
$6.00	$20.00
The Puppet Master	
$6.00	$20.00
Desert Babies	
$6.00	$20.00
He Loved Me Enough To Be Late	
$6.00	$20.00
Out Of The Darkness Into The Light	
$6.00	$20.00
Tell The Devil I Changed My Mind	
$6.00	$20.00
I Am Still In His Hands	
$6.00	$20.00
The Kingdom Is Going To The Dogs	
$6.00	$20.00

MANPOWER: *Healing The Wounded Man Within*
(4 Videos) $60.00
Hidden Mysteries Of The Cross $75.00
(12 Audio Cassettes and Home Study Workbook)
"Woman Thou Art Loosed" Care pack $99.00
(3 Videos, 8 Audios, & 1 Book)

To Order Call Toll Free:

1-800-Bishop-2

Ordering Infomation

Shipping and Handling: $3.95
Overnight Shipments Add: $15
   Please Consider a Love Gift to the Ministry.

Credit Cards Accepted:

☐ **Visa**
☐ **Mastercard**
☐ **American Express**
☐ **Discover**

Card#:_____

Exp. Date:_____

Signture:_____

T.D. Jakes Ministries
P.O. Box 7056
Charleston, WV 25356
1-800-Bishop-2 (247-4672)

how to open the front door while securing the sides and closing the back. • Illustrates Kingdom evangelization and liberation • Amplifies how your church can grow by being qualitatively oriented rather than numerically oriented.

This is My Story $9.95
by Candi Staton

This is My Story is a touching Autobiography about a gifted young child who rose from obscurity and poverty to stardom and wealth. With million-selling albums and a top-charting music career, came a life of heart-brokenness, loneliness and despair. This book will make you both cry and laugh as you witness one woman's search for success and love.

Another Look at Sex $4.95
by Charles Phillips

This book is undoubtedly a head turner and eye opener that will cause you to take another close look at sex. In this book, Charles Phillips openly addresses this seldom discussed subject and giver life-changing advice on sex to married couples and singles. If you have questions about sex, this is the book for you.

Four Laws of Productivity $7.95
by Dr. Mensa Otabil

Success has no favorites. But it does have associates. Success will come to anyone who will pay the price to receive its benefits. *Four Laws of Productivity* will give you four powerful

1 - 8 0 0 - 7 2 7 - 3 2 1 8

keys that will help you achieve your life's goals. *Four Laws of Productivity* by Dr. Mensa Otabil will show you how to: Discover God's gift in you, develop your gift, perfect your gift, and utilized your gift to its maximun potential. The principles revealed in this timely book will radically change your life.

Single Life $7.95

by Earl D. Johnson

A book that candidly addresses the spiritual and physical dimensions of the single life is finally here. Single Life shows the reader how to make their singleness a celebration rather than a burden. This positive approach to singles uses enlightening examples from Apostle Paul, himself a single, to beautifully portray the dynamic aspects of the single life by serving the Lord more effectively. The book gives a fresh light on practical issues such as coping with sexual desires, loneliness and preparation for future mate. Written in a lively style, the author admonishes the singles to seek first the Kingdom of God and rest assured in God's promise to supply their needs.... including a life partner!

Strategies for Saving the Next Generation

by Dave Burrows $5.95

This book will teach you how to start and effectively operate a vibrant youth ministry. This book is filled with practical tips and insight gained over a number of years working with young people from the street to the parks

1 - 8 0 0 - 7 2 7 - 3 2 1 8

to the church. Dave Burrows offers the reader vital information that will produce results if carefully considered and adapted. Excellent for Pastors and Youth Pastor as well as youth workers and those involved with youth ministry.

The Church A Mystery Revealed **$7.95**
by Turnel Nelson

Contrary to the popular and present image of the Church as a religious entity known as Christianity, God's purpose and intent for the Church is that it be an international embassy on earth that represents and manifest the policies, dictates and purposes of the Kingdom of God.

In this book, Pastor Turnel Nelson addresses and outlines some of the fundamental measures that need to be taken in order to revitalize the Church for 21st century evangelism and discipleship.

The Call of God **$7.95**

by Jefferson Edwards

Since I have been called to preach, Now What? Many sincere Christians are confused about their call to the ministry. Some are zealous and run ahead of their time and season of training and preparation while others are behind their time neglecting the gift of God within them. **The Call of God** gives practical instruction for pastors and leaders to refine and further develop their ministry and tips on how to nourish

1 - 8 0 0 - 7 2 7 - 3 2 1 8

and develop others with God's Call to effectively proclaim the gospel of Christ.

The Call of God will help you to: • Have clarity from God as to what ministry involves • Be able to identify and affirm the call in your life • See what stage you are in your call from God • Remove confusion in relation to the processing of a call or the making of the person • Understand the development of the anointing to fulfill your call.

Come, Let Us Pray $6.95
by Emmette Weir

Are you satisfied with your prayer Life? Are you finding that your prayers are often dull, repetitive and lacking in spiritual power? Are you looking for ways to improve your relationship with God? Would you like to be able to pray more effectively? Then *Come, Let Us Pray* will help you in these areas and more. If you want to gain the maximum spiritual experience from your prayer life and enter into the very presence of God. *Come, Let Us Pray.*

Leadership in the New Testament Church
by Earl D. Johnson   **$7.95**

Leadership in the New Testament Church offers practical and applicable insight into the role of leadership in the present day church. In this book, the author explains the qualities that leaders must have, explores the interpersonal relationships between the leader and his staff, the leaders' influence in the church and society

1 - 8 0 0 - 7 2 7 - 3 2 1 8

and how to handle conflicts that arise among leaders.

Becoming A Leader $9.95
by Myles Munroe

Many consider leadership to be no more than staying ahead of the pack, but that is a far cry from what leadership is. Leadership is deploying others to become as good as or better than you are.

Within each of us lies the potential to be an effective leader. **Becoming A Leader** uncovers the secrets of dynamic leadership that will show you how to be a leader in your family, school, community, church and job.

Where ever you are or whatever you do in life this book can help you inevitably become a leader. Remember it is never too late to become a leader. As in every tree there is a forest, so in every follower there is a leader.

Becoming A Leader Workbook $7.95
by Myles Munroe

Now you can activate your leadership potential through the *Becoming A Leader Workbook*. This workbook has been designed to take you step by step through the leadership principles taught in Becoming A Leader. As you participate in the work studies in this workbook you will see the true leader inside you develop and grow into maturity. "Knowledge *with action produces results.*"

1 - 8 0 0 - 7 2 7 - 3 2 1 8

Mobilizing Human Resources $7.95
by Richard Pinder

Pastor Pinder gives an in-depth look at how to organize, motivate and deploy members of the body of Christ in a manner that produces maximum effect for your ministry. This book will assist you in organizing and motivating your 'troops' for effective and efficient ministry. It will also help the individual believer in recognizing their place in the body, using their God given abilities and talents to maximum effect.

The Minister's Topical Bible $14.95
by Derwin Stewart

The Minister's Topical Bible covers every aspect of the ministry providing quick and easy access to scriptures in a variety of ministry related topics. This handy reference tool can be effectively used in leadership training, counseling, teaching, sermon preparation and personal study.

The Believers' Topical Bible
by Derwin Stewart

The Believers' Topical Bible covers every aspect of a Christian's relationship with God and man, providing biblical answers and solutions for all challenges. It is a quick, convenient, and thorough reference Bible that has been designed for use in personal devotions, and group bible studies.   Over 3500 verses that are systematically organized under 240 topics, and is the largest devotional-topical Bible available in NIV and KJV.

New International Version $13.95
King James Version $12.95

1 - 8 0 0 - 7 2 7 - 3 2 1 8